Adapazarı, 2021

3. EDITION

ISBN
978-605-83206-6-6

Translator
Mehmet Lütfi Arslan

Printed by
Erkam Publishing
Phone: +90 212 671 07 00

Publisher
Phone : +90 264 278 9 278
Gsm   : +90 543 278 9 278 (WhatsApp)
info@tomorhoca.com
info@okumayitesvik.com

www.tomorhoca.com

THE KORAN
AND
THE BIBLE

*

AHMET TOMOR

CONTENTS

Preface 7

What I Was - What I Became - What Will I Be 13

What Is Spiritual Training? 21

The True Religion And The Divine Book 23

The Characteristics Of The Divine Book 24

The Divine Book And The Prophets 25

The History Of The Bible 27

The History Of The Qur'an 36

The Characteristics Of The Divine Book And
The Bible 44

The True And Real Bible 50

Was Prophet Jesus Really Crucified? 57

If The True Bible Is Found What Will Happen? 68

The Characteristics Of The Divine Book And
The Qur'an 71

A Comparison Of The Qur'an And The Bible 74

The Qur'an And Prophet Muhammad 80

The Qur'an Cannot Be The Word Of Prophet Muhammad 86

The Spirituality Of The Qur'an 88

Islamic Civilization 91

The First Social Activity Of Islamic State: Masjid 93

Human Rights And Islam 99

PREFACE

Infinite praise be to Allah who is the Lord of all universes and gratitude to Prophet Muhammad who everlastingly prays, "my Ummah, my Ummah" and to his companions.

My dear readers!

Prophet Muhammad, the true defender of human rights, who abolished discrimination based on race, color or language said in his last sermon:

"O people! Your Lord is one. Your father is one, too. You are all Adam's children and Adam is from the earth. Your superiority in the eyes of Allah is according to piety and good action."

Our dear Prophet warned us to have four characteristics if we want to live in peace and harmony, whatever our race, language or belief:

1- Your Lord is one.

Our Lord is Allah, without any discrimination based on race, color or language, and we are all His servants.

There is no god other than Allah. He has created the material world and all creation beyond the material world, establishing the balance of this universe by placing the earth, the sun, the stars and the galaxies in their orbits.

The nature and commonsense of humanity requires that Allah is the One.

Associating partners with Allah by idolizing humans, stones or statutes is contradictory to the nature and commonsense of humanity. It causes disturbance and divisions in society.

2- Your Father is one; all of you are the sons of Adam.

With no difference based on race, color, language or genes, Adam is the father of us all; we are all Adam's children.

Since all people descend from Adam and all of them are his children and grandchildren, they are all brothers and sisters in blood. Disagreements and disputes among them are irrelevant, even if they differ in terms of race, color, language or belief.

3- Adam is from the earth.

Our origin is the earth, because our father Prophet Adam was created from the elements of the earth.

We walk over the surface of the earth and it accepts everything in its bosom. It is the symbol of modesty and humility. It is the nature of humans. Therefore, arrogance, ridiculing people and mocking them are all opposed to the nature of the earth and therefore are foreign to human nature. People and society deem all of these to be unpleasant.

If we think fairly, we can understand that humans are not for nothing, because as our arrival on this earth was not according to our will, our life in this earth and our death (how, when and where) is not according to our will either.

We can determine neither the elements that make up our body, nor the conditions (which age, country or race) under which we live. So is there any difference between black children born in Africa and white children born in Europe?

4- Your superiority in the eyes of Allah is according to *taqwa*.

The superiority of humans in the eyes of Allah is not according to their birth of place, be it Asia, Africa, Europe or America, but according to their *taqwa* (piety).

What is *taqwa*?

Taqwa comes from the word *viqaya*, which means protection and abstinence.

Taqwa means completely abstaining from sins through the fear of Allah and performing good deeds. Those who have *taqwa* are called *muttaqeen*.

The *muttaqeen* are the worthiest people in the eyes of Allah. Paradise is for them.

Allah Almighty does not look at a person's race, country, language or color, but at the *taqwa* in their hearts.

Our Prophet, pointing at his heart three times said: "*Taqwa* is here, *taqwa* is here, *taqwa* is here," stressing that *taqwa* is a function of the heart.

Having *taqwa* is a kind of *noor* (light) and its place is inn the heart. If one abstains from sins and performs their prayers at their predetermined times, this *noor* of *taqwa* is enhanced and one gets peace.

Otherwise, this *noor* becomes weak and the heart begins to blacken. When one's heart is blackened, that person falls into hard times, suffering stress and spiritual depression.

The perception of the concepts of sin and praying may change from time to time, from country to country or even from people to people. Yet, this is not good for humanity. The important thing is to perform the deeds and abstain from the sins manifested in the true religion of Allah and its divine book.

✻ ✻ ✻

My Dear Readers!

Every era has different religions in addition to the true religion, as is the case for today. In this book, I try to explain the true religion and the divine book as far as I can in order for you to understand the true religion in the eyes of Allah and its main source, the divine book and to reach spiritual peace in this world and Paradise and at *Jamalullah* (the face of Allah) in the Hereafter.

Guidance is from Allah and effort is from all of us.

WHAT I WAS
WHAT I BECAME
WHAT WILL I BE
❋

Our forefathers said: "Do not say what I was, instead say what I will be."

However, since those who do not learn from the lessons of their past are unable to project their future, let us first examine our past, and then we will look at our future.

What Was I?

There were visitors to this world before us. We were dead elements, existing as oxygen, hydrogen, nitrogen, carbon, potassium, calcium, sodium, phosphorus, magnesium and iron. It could have lasted forever like that.

Yet, Allah, the Lord of all universes, can do whatever He wishes.

As He can transform dead elements into living organisms and creatures, He can also do the reverse.

No one can stop Him and no one can alter the laws set by Him as there is no partner who can be associated with Him.

While we were dead elements in the ground, Allah poured abundant rain over us. We could not bear it. We were dissolved and became clay.

We were absorbed by the roots of the plants and transformed into , and are called cereal, fruit, and vegetables.

We were digested in those who had consumed us and transformed into reproductive cells, and known as sperm and ova.

When we were fertilized by the will of Allah, we were known as the embryo and when our organs were shaped, we were called fetuses.

When we were able to accord with the conditions of the earth, we were born as small humans, and called **infants**.

What Did I Become?

How did we come from "What I was" to "What I Became" and what phases did we pass through?

Let us go as far back as we can remember in order to learn this lesson.

Once we were babies who used to cry, breastfeed, snivel and wet ourselves. Then we grew up and became the darlings of our parents.

In the material world, everything is in action and in the process of change; we are dependent on the laws of this world. We could have ended up not the darlings of our parents.

For some time, we played and then we studied. After graduating from primary school, middle school, and finally high school, we found ourselves in universities or embarked on a career.

Meanwhile, we were growing up physically and emotionally. We became youngsters full of energy and dynamic.

O Lord! Where did those days pass away to? Only yesterday we were the darlings of our parents.

Then, we became engaged and married. We had husbands or wives, and homes and children.

Then we got status, power and authority. Our circle became ever larger and our lives became enriched. We reached the pinnacle. Then our stagnation period began.

While activity continues in the material world and our life continues, we cannot last forever!

When we look at behind us, we see a signboard reading "No Return."

We have no choice but to descend from the pinnacle and to continue to run in the race of life.

When we look down from the top, we see a great graveyard surrounded by those who were buried before us.

We begin to descend to the graveyard. What will happen now? When our lives are over, will we be buried in a hole?

O Lord! Is our life an illusion? Will our bodies combine with the ground?

If so, then what is the hurry to reach the top? Why do we tire ourselves out? Why all this effort? In other words, why did we join a marathon if the result is already known?

What Will I Be?

Even though times change, new galaxies are discovered, man takes steps on the moon and computer networks turn the world into an office, the race of humanity continues towards death and one day the Angel of Death will take our souls. We will be buried in pits dug in the graveyards by our friends.

That day, we will understand that our worldly life was nothing but an illusion; it will be as if it has never been lived and our bodies will decay and become ground.

At this point one may ask a question:

A living organism, say a flower, also decays and becomes ground. If so, what is the difference between a human and a flower or a piece of straw?

Humans, of course, are fundamentally different from plants, ants, elephants and birds.

Because Allah says:

"We have indeed created man in the best of molds." (At-Tin, 4)

The human, created in the best form anatomically and physically, becomes aware with their mind and limited by the soul. They are the caliphate (sovereign) on the earth and candidates for Paradise, the place of infinity.

Humans are the only creation whose head is upright and who walks straight on two feet.

Humans are the only creation that can eat the best of food by cutting, washing, cooking and serving one another.

Humans are the only creation that can talk, tell their ideas concisely, listen to others and benefit from the knowledge of others.

Humans are the only creation that can take advantage of previous experiences through reading and writing, make progress in science and technology by adding them to their own experiences.

Since the human has many material and spiritual capabilities, surely they are not the same as a flower or piece of straw.

* * *

The human is the only creation that comprises all of the universe, be it material or beyond material.

They are physically dependent upon the material universe and spiritually dependent upon the universe that is beyond the material. While their dead body decays like a flower, their spiritual entity continues to live after its demise.

Physical diseases, permanent handicaps and social turmoil temporarily affect the soul. Likewise, death is also a shock to it. Yet, after a while, the soul overcomes the shock of death and it becomes reconciled to the universe of *Barzakh*.

According to the life and belief of the person in the world, they either face torment in the grave, which becomes one of the pits of the pits of Hell, or they are spiritually content there when it becomes a garden from the gardens of Paradise.

The Soul and Body

The true and permanent character of the human is the soul. There is no spiritual difference between the 20-year old and the 70-

year old. Nevertheless, the 20-year old cannot perform the same actions with an old body and the 70-year old cannot perform the same actions with a 20-year old body. A soul who resides in the universe of *Barzakh* cannot perform what has been done in the world because the body has decayed and gone.

Why do we come to this world if our life ends with death? More truly why were we sent?

In fact, we did not come by our will!

As small woods would be restrictive to a lion, which was created for great forests and a lake would limit the whale, created for oceans, Allah has created the human for paradise, and thus, the world limits us.

This world is as narrow and confined as the uterus is compared to the earth.

Yet, in the same way that we have to stay in the uterus for a limited time for the sake of our physical development, we have to stay in this world in order to reach spiritual maturity and thereby gain Paradise.

WHAT IS SPIRITUAL TRAINING?

The form of education which is stored in the cells of brain and which is useless after the death of brain, having no benefit for spiritual maturity is called worldly education.

The education which helps humans to live peacefully and healthily and to gain Paradise is called spiritual education.

The basic source of spiritual education is the True Religion, its teacher is the Prophet, and its curriculum is the Divine Book.

Other belief systems apart from this, which are not based on the True Religion and the Divine Book, whether they are called religions or not, are null and void. They are worthless in the eyes of Allah.

Beginning from ancient times, every age has had its own perverted beliefs that are opposed to the True Religion. The adherents of these perverted beliefs have terrorized the countries in which they dominated, and coerced their people to accept their perverted beliefs.

In fact, the struggle between right and wrong, which began with Adam and Satan, still continues globally. If this is so, how do humans reach the True Religion by overcoming perverted beliefs?

As harmful and edible plants are mixed together in the grasslands, it is natural that right and wrong are mixed together in this world, as it is the testing ground for the Hereafter.

While the animals, which have no reason, avoid harmful plants and eat edible ones, it is the duty of humans who have been embellished with mind and who are candidates for the Paradise, to overcome perverted beliefs and find the True Religion for their future.

The mind can help us in this regard if we use it properly; the mind is connected to volition like a projector. As a projector lights up the area to which it is directed, the mind also is lightened by the direction in which it aims, searches, and is interested. This is so that humans might become experts in those subjects; they are ignorant of that in which they are not interested.

THE TRUE RELIGION AND THE DIVINE BOOK

*

The right (Haq), the opposite of wrong, is only the truth. Because Allah says:

> *"What is there after the truth but error?"*
> *(Yunus, 32)*

The belief systems other than the True Religion, even though they are called religions, are perverted beliefs. The real and valid religion in the eyes of Allah is the True Religion.

The True Religion is the divine religion and its main source is the divine book.

My Dear Readers!

Religion is not a means of entertainment like sports. Religion is a necessity and the future of humans is dependent upon it.

Let us direct our mind projector to the divine book, the main source of the True Religion and examine the characteristics that are required of a divine book.

THE CHARACTERISTICS OF THE DIVINE BOOK
*

1- The divine book should not be contradictory to the attribute "divine". It should only belong to Allah and not contain one single word belonging to anyone other than Allah.

2- The divine book should keep its original language as it was sent to the prophet and this book should be the main source of the religion.

3- The divine book should maintain its syntax, that is, the arrangement of words, as determined by Allah.

Sometimes the change of a word, a letter or even a comma might cause the opposite meaning to appear.

For example;

Read like your father, do not be foolish

Read; like your father do not be foolish.

THE DIVINE BOOK AND
THE PROPHETS
✳

The prophets are spiritual pioneers appointed by Allah who have the ability to understand, perform and teach the Divine Book in the direction of the divine will.

The words of the prophets other than those in the divine book are called *Hadith*.

Hadiths are generally explanations of the divine book. However, they should not be confused with the divine book, as their meanings and syntax are human and not divine.

After explaining the most fundamental characteristics of the divine books, let us examine the situations of the Qur'an and the New Testament, examine how they have reached us and understand which one has preserved the characteristics of a divine book. These two books are sources of two major religions, Islam and Christianity, both of both is in the spotlight in terms of civilizational and interfaith dialogue.

An important warning!

Since I, the writer of this book, am a Muslim, let me remind my dear readers who may prejudge me, supposing that I will praise the Qur'an and criticize the New Testament, that both two important principals of Islamic belief.

Muslims believe in all the prophets, without differentiating between them. We also believe in all the divine books without differentiating between them.

While some Christian fanatics insult Prophet Muhammad and the Qur'an, we mention Prophet Jesus with salutations and greetings and respect the original Bible in the same way that we respect the Qur'an.

THE HISTORY OF THE BIBLE
*

Prophet Jesus was a son of Israel. When his mother Mary, who was a sinless virgin, gave birth to him by the will of Allah, the Jews declared this birth illegitimate and attempted to kill Jesus and his mother.

Jesus became a prophet at the age of 30 and Allah revealed the Bible to him. At the age of 33, Allah raised Jesus up to Himself. So his prophecy lasted for just three years.

Prophet Jesus preached the religion of Allah in secrecy because of the hostility of the Jews. He had very few believers, including the twelve disciples, known as *hawariyun*, in his three years of prophecy.

Prophet Jesus spread the word of Allah under very difficult conditions. He educated his twelve disciples, who assisted him in preaching. They spiritually reached the highest ranks through private conversations with Prophet

Jesus. After Allah had raised Jesus up, the disciples began to spread Christianity, the only religion of Allah at that time, in secrecy, by going to different parts of the world.

However, while Prophet Jesus knew the Bible completely, the disciples only knew some parts of it. None of them could memorize all of it. Moreover, when they went to different parts of the world, they did not have the Bible, the source book of what they were preaching, with them.

The disciples were preaching Christianity to people, usually meeting with them in secret, dark cellars, because of the oppression of the Roman Empire.

The disciples, who were admirers of Prophet Jesus, spoke of their memories of him, as well as reciting parts of the Bible and giving advice to people.

Those who had been with the disciples and could read and write began to record what they had heard, but not in an organized form; this eventually came to be known as the Bible, or New Testament.

Since each of these people had a different understanding and ability to write, some versions of the New Testament, which were different from others or inconsistent, began to emerge.

This trend continued for some time. The succeeding adherents attempted to rewrite the so-called new Bibles, quoting first the manuscripts from which were written on dried leathers, but again, not in an organized order. Thus, hundreds of new books, inconsistent with each other and containing a multitude of stories and legends, became widespread, known as Bibles.

The Christians were perplexed. On the one hand, they had a cruel enemy, the Roman Empire breathing down their necks, while on the other hand, they had different and contradictory books all known as divine books; add to this the monks who claimed that only their versions were the original Bible and we can understand the situation better.

In 330 AD shocking news was heard throughout the Roman Empire. Constantine the Great had converted to Christianity. The people could not believe what they heard. The sole ruler of a great empire, the merciless enemy of Christianity, had become a believer. The news was true. First, the persecution of the Christians came to a halt and then Christianity was declared as the imperial state religion of the Roman Empire.

Yet, the confusion of different Bibles still continued. The Christians believe that Constantine the Great was the only man who could solve this problem, because he was the sole ruler of his time, and had built a great city on seven hills with impassable great walls around it known as Constantinople.

Constantine the Great convoked the First Council of Nicea in 325 and invited more than 300 priests. The priests, coming from different parts of the Roman Empire, were to resolve the disagreements between hundreds of different gospels and to approve one text as being the true Bible, while discarding the others.

This was the goal of Constantine, yet it was too late; Prophet Jesus had been taken up to Heaven 292 years before and the disciples had also passed away many years ago. Many things had happened since that time, many generations had passed and numerous books called the Bible had emerged.

There was another situation of which Constantine the Great was not aware. Until he had become sole ruler, the Christians had been persecuted and every type of religious activity had been strictly forbidden. There had been no religious institutes in which priests or monks could be educated.

Those priests that were invited to the First Council of Nicea were not registered or educated. They had had no formal religious education. They were untrained people who defended their own gospels as the word of God.

The outcome of the Council was clear before it even began. Discussions would take place and every priest would defend his own Gospel, but then what?

Of course, the gospel or the gospels of those priests that were backed by Constantine the

Great would be approved and the disagreements would be resolved.

Constantine initiated an error that would have repercussions until the Day of Judgment. But he had no other choice. His attempt was a historical gamble. Unfortunately, this gamble did not pay off, and everybody lost.

After long discussions, the gospels backed by Constantine; that is, Matthew, Mark, Luke and John, were approved as being the true Bible. To these were added "The Acts of Apostles", which, it was claimed, had been written by Luke and some epistles written by others. It was also decided that any other texts were to be destroyed.

Yet, there was no unanimous decision. Those who opposed the decision were threatened. For instance, Arius, who was against the decision, was threatened with excommunication and then death. Even though he fled to Egypt this did not help him to survive and he was killed.

Constantine's iron fist could not stop the confusion of the gospels and it did not satisfy the conscience of the Christians themselves.

After Constantine's death, the confusion of gospels arose again and another council was held in Laodicea in 364 AD. This council made some changes, announcing them to the public, but it did not solve the problem. In 397, the Council of Carthage was held for the same purpose. If a book is a divine book, not even a comma can be changed. Nevertheless, the changes made to the New Testament continued at different times in councils held in Istanbul, Izmir, Aydin, Ephesus, and Chalcedon.

Let me state an explanation that springs from my heart:

While trying to explain historical facts regarding the writing of the New Testament, I became very worried and distressed about Prophet Jesus and the True Bible.

Constantine the Great came to mind. When he converted to Christianity, he was faced with the fact that there were hundreds of gospels that were inconsistent and contradictory with one another. Probably, he was more worried than me and soon invited the priests to resolve this problem. He could lessen the number of the gospels to four, yet he could not end the confusion. He was not able to do so.

Christian believers who cannot answer the question of *'Why are there four gospels?'* try to cover the truth that there is more than one New Testament and they deny that the Council of Nicea occurred.

I advise them to read the beginning of Luke:

Luke: 1.1: O Theophilus, forasmuch as many have taken in hand to set forth in order a narration of the things that have been accomplished among us,

Yes, according to Luke, many began to narrate. What about the others that Luke did not know of?

"The Encyclopedia of Religion and Ethics' (Vol. 2, p. 582) says: "Jesus neither left a scripture nor gave any order to his disciples to write anything down."

There is no evidence that Matthew, Mark, Luke or John were the authors of their gospels. The original language of the New Testament is Hebrew. Hebrew scripts of these four gospels still cannot be found. Nor are the identities of the translators into Latin and Greek known.

THE HISTORY OF THE QUR'AN

*

The last prophet, Prophet Muhammad was born in Mecca. He became prophet at the age of 40. He continued to receive revelation for 23 years, 13 years of this in Mecca and 10 years in Medina.

Prophet Muhammad, the last messenger of Allah, received the first verses of the Qur'an, the last divine book, on Mount Hira. The revelation of the Qur'an was completed in 23 years.

Since the Qur'an is the last divine book, it is natural that it has different characteristics from earlier books. One of these characteristics is that the Qur'an is under the protection of Allah.

Allah Almighty says:

"Surely We have revealed the Reminder and We will most surely be its guardian."
(Al-Hijr, 9)

The Qur'an, because of being under the protection of Allah, will not be corrupted, no word of it will be changed and it will last and be valid until the Day of Judgment, as its language has been preserved as it descended to Prophet Muhammad.

At times, the hostility towards the Qur'an launched by Abu Jahl turned into a state terror. Yet, nobody was able to change a word of it, as we will see below. While the enemies of the Qur'an have decayed under the ground, the book has stood as it was sent for some 1,400 years.

Another characteristic of the Qur'an is that while other divine books were revealed only once to their prophets, the Qur'an was revealed in surahs and ayats, and took a total of 23 years to be revealed.

Prophet Muhammad had the revelations immediately recorded by scribes. Then, he dictated them to the people around, word by word, usually repeating the relevant ayat three times.

Those who heard the new revelations from Prophet Muhammad spread what they had learned and conveyed the message to those who were not present.

While the literate companions memorized the new ayats from the text, the illiterate ones listened and thus memorized them.

The revelation of the Qur'an in terms of short pieces like ayats and surahs and over a long period of 23 years ensured that every ayat was written down, memorized, understood and applied to daily life, and thus the Muslims confirmed with the messages of the Qur'an.

There was no possibility for any ayat to be forgotten, because every ayat was recited in the daily prayers. The Qur'an was part of the daily lives of the Muslims. All aspects of their personal and social lives, beliefs, even the way they ate, drank, got married and inherited were regulated according to the Qur'an. Even children playing in the streets warned their friends if they did not behave properly.

Prophet Muhammad applied the Qur'an in his daily life, caused it to be written down and memorized word by word, and conveyed its message by reciting it in daily, Jum'a and festival prayers; later he asked his companions three times: "Did I convey it to you properly?" The companions responded: "Yes." Upon this, he lifted his hands and said: "Witness, o Lord!"

Prophet Muhammad passed away in the month of *Rabi-al Awwal* after his return from pilgrimage.

After passing away from this world to the Hereafter, the prophethood finished and the period of the caliphs began. The caliphs were entitled to carry on the Islamic state and convey the message of the Qur'an and Sunnah to coming generations.

While Prophet Muhammad lived the revelation continued, only to be finished near the end of his life.

At the time of Abu Bakr, 70 people who had memorized the Qur'an were martyred at the battle of Yamama. Umar was concerned for the future of the Qur'an. In fact, this was not an issue at that time, as there were thousands of companions and scribes who had fully or partly memorized the Qur'an. Yet, what would happen after them? They would die, as well. This was the concern of Umar.

Umar expressed his concern to Abu Bakr and stressed that while thousands of companions and scribes were still alive, the ayats and surahs should be written in a certain order and turned into a complete book.

Abu Bakr shared this concern. It would be dangerous to wait for this vital task to be completed by coming generations. After some consultation, he requested that a commission be formed and Zaid Ibn Thabit was to head this commission.

Who was Zaid Ibn Thabit?

Zaid was one who had memorized the Qur'an and who had written the divine revelation down.

He was from the Ansars (those who lived in Medina). He converted to Islam at the age of 11 before the Hijra (emigration) at the invitation of Mus'ab Al Umayr. Assisting Mus'ab, he had memorized all the ayats he heard from him and taught them to the children of Medina.

After the Hijra, he became the scribe of the Prophet as his handwriting was very good. He not only recorded divine revelations, but also managed official correspondence.

After the Islamic State had been recognized by other states, Prophet Muhammad began to receive letters from foreign statesmen. These needed to be translated into Arabic and answered.

Prophet Muhammad asked Zaid, who had a good memory, to learn Hebrew and Syriac. Taking the Prophet's wish as a sacred duty, Zaid learned these two languages well in a short time.

The Commission

The commission headed by Zaid Ibn Thabit began to work according to the instructions of the Caliphate:

a- The Commission's work would be open to public and anybody who wished to observe the work of the commission would be free to do so.

b- No ayat that had been memorized would be accepted unless it was certified.

c- Only written text that had two witnesses to testify that it had been written as dictated by the Prophet in their presence would be accepted. They ayats must have been memorized as well.

d- The surahs would be placed in order according to the order dictated by Prophet Muhammad, not the order of revelation.

After a long and spiritually accountable work, the commission completed its job and finished the compilation of the Qur'an, the last divine book. The original copy was bonded and presented for the companions to examine.

It was examined again and again, and approved unanimously by tens of thousands of companions. This Qur'an was called the *Umm al-Mushaf* (Mother Qur'an) and delivered to Abu Bakr on behalf of the caliphate.

During the caliphate of Uthman, the boundaries of Islamic State were broadened. Huzaifa, who participated in the conquest of Azerbaijan and Armenia, told Uthman after his return:

"I suggest you send the copies of the original Qur'an to some Islamic cities to make sure that

new converts to Islam and those far away from
Medina may benefit from 'Umm al-Mushaf.'

Uthman asked that another commission be formed, again headed by Zaid Ibn Thabit. This commission made copies of the original Qur'an and sent them to certain cities.

THE CHARACTERISTICS OF THE DIVINE BOOK AND THE BIBLE

*

First a warning:

Adherence to religion is in no way akin to supporting a favorite sports team. Therefore, people cannot easily abandon their attachments to their religions, be they are true or false.

The Prophets were frequently told by people "We cannot abandon what our fathers left to us."

Should people follow the way their fathers once followed? For instance, must a man whose father was poor live poorly? Must a man whose father was a shepherd be a shepherd? Finally, must a man whose father followed a wrong way follow the same way?

Of course not, as we know from life. Many poor children have become rich people and many children whose fathers were shepherds have become governors and statesmen.

Likewise, many children whose fathers were on the wrong path have become the most idealistic and powerful defenders of the true religion.

✳ ✳ ✳

The clearest and most distinct characteristic of a divine book is its language.

A divine book should preserve its original language as it was revealed to its prophet. If this is so, it can keep its status of being a divine book and the source of religion. Otherwise, it loses this status.

The original language of the Bible revealed to Prophet Jesus was Hebrew. Unfortunately, true Bible has been lost, since the diligence, care and spirit of cooperation in the collection and memorization of the Qur'an was not or could not be manifested in the collection and memorization of the Bible.

The New Testament which has been recited in churches and distributed by missionaries for centuries consists of versions, selected among controversy from among hundreds of Bibles in 325 by the Nicea Consulate.

Another characteristic of the divine book is that its syntax and word order should be as Allah has assigned.

When we look at the verse *Alhamdu lillahi Rabbil alamin,* if we change the place of any word, say *Alhamdu,* then we change the syntax that Allah determined and this negates its character of divinity.

Let me give two examples from the New Testament in order to be clear. These examples are from Matthew and Mark, concerned with same topic and having the same title:

MATTHEW; *"Jesus Heals Many"* (8-14)

When Jesus came into Peter's house, he saw Peter's mother-in-law lying in bed with a fever. 15 He touched her hand and the fever left her, and she got up and began to wait on him.

MARK; *"Jesus Heals Many"* (29-39)

As soon as they left the synagogue, they went with James and John to the home of Simon and Andrew. Simon's mother-in-law was in bed with a fever, and they told Jesus about her. So he went to her, took her hand and helped her up. The fever left her and she began to wait on them.

While not one word of a divine book should be changed, these two examples exhibit many omissions, additions and changes.

If one of these versions is true, then the other is false; if one is correct then the other is wrong. Unfortunately, these two examples are from the modern Bible and are recited as the word of God in churches and ceremonies.

Another striking example is concerned with the genealogy of Jesus.

MATTHEW;
"The Genealogy of Jesus" (1-17)
"Abraham was the father of Isaac, Isaac the father of Jacob."

Matthew begins by giving the genealogy of Jesus dating from Abraham as *"Abraham was the father of Isaac"* and ending up with Joseph, the son of Jacob: *"Matthan the father of Jacob, and Jacob the father of Joseph, the husband of Mary, of whom was born Jesus, who is called Christ."*

LUKE; *"The Genealogy of Jesus" (23-38)*

Now Jesus himself was about thirty years old when he began his ministry. He was the son, so it was thought, of Joseph, the son of Heli…"

Luke, as opposed to Matthew, begins from Joseph, the son of Heli and goes back to Adam, and calling Adam the son of God.

"The son of Enosh, the son of Seth, the son of Adam, the son of God."

Apart from additions, omissions and changes, one of these two texts says that Jesus is the grandson of Heli, while the other states that he is the grandson of Jacob, with both stating that his father was Joseph.

The whole world, except the Jews, knew that Jesus was born without a father and had only one grandfather. This was his mother's father, Imran. And Jesus' genealogy can only be traced down this line.

Unfortunately, these contradictory texts are recited as the holy book in churches.

When I saw the contradictions in today's Bible, I thought about Surah Al-Fatiha. If one attempts to compare the Qur'an that was written centuries ago and the Qur'an printed today by looking only at Surah Al-Fatiha, there is no difference, it always begins with *"Alhamdu"* and ends up with *"Waladdâllin."*

The most crucial characteristic of the divine book is that it belongs to Allah Almighty. There should be no additions, not even one word, to the divine book by a person. When we evaluate this situation free from bias, we can understand that this is a prerequisite of logic and reason. While people protect their books from plagiarism and change by copyright, how can we think that Allah is not able to protect His Book and that He will not punish the wrong-doers.

As Allah Almighty, the Lord of all the universes and the only Sovereign of the earth and heavens, does not allow anyone to interfere with His acts, so too will He not allow His Book to be changed. For instance, the word "Amen" has not been added to the Qur'an, because it not the word of Allah, but rather the practice of the Prophet after reciting Surah Al-Fatiha.

THE TRUE AND REAL BIBLE
*

Muslims believe that the Bible that was revealed to Prophet Jesus was a genuine revelation and that it was the same divine book that they believe the Qur'an to be.

However, the New Testament of the Bible today consists of 27 sections written by different writers at different times. Only fanatics can call such book a divine book.

The New Testament consists of four parts:

1- The Gospels, written by Matthew, Mark, Luke and John. (These Gospels form the essence of the Bible and Christianity.)

2- The Acts of the Apostles.

3- The Epistles of Paul, Peter, John, Joseph and Judas.

4- The Revelation.

1- The Gospels of Matthew, Mark, Luke and John.

Luke begins with the following:

LUKE; (1-3)

"Many have undertaken to draw up an account of the things that have been fulfilled among us, just as they were handed down to us by those who from the first were eyewitnesses and servants of the word. Therefore, since I myself have carefully investigated everything from the beginning, it seemed good also to me to write an orderly account for you, most excellent Theophilus, so that you may know the certainty of the things you have been taught."

Luke begins with "most excellent Theophilus", not the name of Allah/God. This is normal, because he is not writing the true Bible, but an account of things that happened among the early Christians. He addresses Theophilus, stating that he is to convey the testimonies of eyewitnesses.

This is all very normal. What comes next?

It is very interesting that these texts are recited in churches as the word of God written by Luke.

What would be Luke's reaction be to this?

A preface of the Bible published by the Corporation of the Holy Book and printed by Orhan Printing in 1998 reports:

"The New Testament (Contemporary Bible) consists of twenty-seven different articles. They focus on four general topics and are consistent. The life of Jesus was narrated by four writers, Matthew, Mark, Luke and John. They not only witnessed the events but also received the testimonies of other witnesses."

As this text expresses, Matthew, Mark, and John, like Luke, were not claiming that they were writing a holy book but rather that they were conveying the memories and testimonies of other witnesses about the life of Prophet Jesus. It was natural for them to convey what had happened in the time of Prophet Jesus, as this is the way history and historians work. Hence, the writings of Matthew, Mark, Luke and John should be regarded as historical texts.

However, others lost true Bible and embraced these texts as divine books, turning them into the main source of Christianity. One cannot argue that these four writers conveyed accurate and complete information about the time of Prophet Isa, because even historians, who study the same subject and who are dependent on scientific findings can find contradictions. If so, it is natural that there are contradictions between these four writers.

✱✱✱

In the section "A General View of the Bible", I have already given examples regarding the writings of these four authors. Let me give some examples from the conclusions of their writings.

MATTHEW;

"Judas Agrees to Betray Jesus" (14-16)

Then one of the Twelve—the one called Judas Iscariot—went to the chief priests and asked, "What are you willing to give me if I hand him over to you?" So they counted out for him thirty silver coins.

LUKE; *"Judas Agrees to Betray Jesus"* (3-6)

Now the Feast of Unleavened Bread, called the Passover, was approaching, and the chief priests and the teachers of the law were looking for some way to get rid of Jesus, for they were afraid of the people. Then Satan entered Judas, called Iscariot, one of the Twelve. And Judas went to the chief priests and the officers of the temple guard and discussed with them how he might betray Jesus. They were delighted and agreed to give him money.

MARK; *"Jesus Arrested"* (44-47)

Now the betrayer had arranged a signal with them: "The one I kiss is the man; arrest him and lead him away under guard." 45 Going at once to Jesus, Judas said, "Rabbi!" and kissed him. 46 The men seized Jesus and arrested him. 47 Then one of those standing near drew his sword and struck the servant of the high priest, cutting off his ear.

JOHN; *"Jesus Arrested"* (18-3)

So Judas came to the grove, guiding a detachment of soldiers and some officials from the chief priests and Pharisees. They were carrying torches, lanterns and weapons. Jesus, knowing *all that was going to happen to him, went out and asked them, "Who is it you want?" "Jesus of Nazareth," they replied. "I am he," Jesus said. And Judas the traitor was standing there with them. When Jesus said, "I am he," they drew back and fell to the ground.*

My dear readers, no comment is necessary here, as the many contradictions are so apparent.

Let us look at the legend of the crucifixion of Prophet Jesus.

MATTHEW; *"The Crucifixion"* (27-32)

As they were going out, they met a man from Cyrene, named Simon, and they forced him to carry the cross. They came to a place called Golgotha (which means The Place of the Skull). There they offered Jesus wine to drink, mixed with gall; but after tasting it, he refused to drink it. When they had crucified him, they divided up his clothes by casting lots.

JOHN; *"The Crucifixion"* (19-17)

Carrying his own cross, Jesus went out to the place of the Skull (which in Aramaic is called Golgotha). Here they crucified him, and with him two others—one on each side and Jesus in the middle."

MARCUS; *"The Death of Jesus"* (15-33)

At the sixth hour darkness came over the whole land until the ninth hour. And at the ninth hour Jesus cried out in a loud voice, "Eloi, Eloi, lama sabachthani?"—which means, "My God, my God, why have you forsaken me?" With a loud cry, Jesus breathed his last.

JOHN; *"The Death of Jesus"* (15-33)

Later, knowing that all was now completed, and so that the Scripture would be fulfilled, Jesus said, "I am thirsty." A jar of wine vinegar was there, so they soaked a sponge in it, put the sponge on a stalk of the hyssop plant, and lifted it to Jesus' lips. When he had received the drink, Jesus said, "It is finished." With that, he bowed his head and gave up his spirit.

WAS PROPHET JESUS REALLY CRUCIFIED?

According to the Church, yes he was crucified, as this is what is recorded in the Bible.

Who wrote this in the Bible? The arrest, interrogation, and execution of Jesus have no relation to the genuine revelation. Divine books were revealed to real prophets. So were divine messages. So how do we know that Jesus cried, saying, "*Eli, Eli lama sabachthani*" or "I am thirsty" while being crucified. It is thought that a false prophet added these words to the Bible. If these words were the confessions of witnesses, then we would be justified in asking whether the New Testament is a historical record or a divine book.

Who were the people who added these false words to the Bible?

The crucifixion of Prophet Jesus, a man who changed life drastically, is still an enigma for scholars of religion and history. The Church transformed it into a symbol of Christianity, regarding the wearing of the cross as a form of worship. This is something unheard of before in western civilization.

So, what was behind this event?

The only reliable source that clarifies this event is the last divine book, the Qur'an:

Allah Almighty says:

"And their saying: Surely we have killed the Messiah, Jesus son of Mary, the messenger of Allah; but they did not kill him nor did they crucify him, but it appeared to them so (like Jesus) and most surely those who differ therein are only in a doubt about it; they have no knowledge respecting it, but only follow a conjecture, and they killed him not for sure. Nay! Allah took him up to Himself; and Allah is Mighty, Wise." (An-Nisa, 157-158)

Allah Almighty not only clarifies the event of crucifixion, but also removes doubts about it.

Yes, Prophet Jesus was neither killed nor crucified.

One of the disciples, Judas betrayed him for money and guided the soldiers to Prophet Jesus. At that time, there was great confusion. Allah raised Jesus to heaven and transformed Judas into the body of Jesus. The soldiers arrested Judas and nobody believed his denial when he called out "I am not Jesus." Those who arrested, questioned and crucified Judas later wondered whether it had really been Jesus or not, because even though the face of Judas was similar to that of Jesus, his body was completely different. They were perplexed and asked: "If this is Jesus, where is Judas? If this is Judas, where is Jesus?"

What happened to Judas?

According to Islam, he was crucified in Jesus' stead and killed.

What does Christianity say?

MATTHEW;

"Judas Hangs Himself." (27-3)

When Judas, who had betrayed him, saw that Jesus was condemned, he was seized with remorse and returned the thirty silver coins to the chief priests and the elders. "I have sinned," he said, "for I have betrayed innocent blood." "What is that to us?" they replied. "That's your responsibility." So Judas threw the money into the temple and left. Then he went away and hanged himself.

Acts of Apostles

"Matthias Chosen to Replace Judas" (1-18)

He was one of our numbers and shared in this ministry. "With the reward he got for his wickedness, Judas bought a field; there he fell headlong, his body burst open and all his intestines spilled out. Everyone in Jerusalem heard about this.

According to Matthew, Judas was seized with remorse, returned the silver coins that had been given to him for his betrayal and hanged himself.

According to Acts of Apostles, Judas bought a field with the silver he received for his betrayal, fell headlong there and his body burst open, with all his intestines spilling out.

An important remark:

I do not want to be misunderstood. Judas did not fall off a plane. He fell in his field which he had bought with the money he had been paid for his betrayal. Upon this, his body burst open and all his intestines spilled out. Everyone in Jerusalem heard about this, except poor Matthew, who conveyed the event otherwise.

My dear readers!

These confusing narrations are recited as parts of the holy book in churches; they are listened to by western intellectuals and marketed as holy books by missionaries in Islamic countries.

What actually happened to Prophet Jesus?

According to Islam, he was neither crucified nor killed. Allah Almighty raised him to heaven alive.

According to the Christians:

MATTHEW; *"The Burial of Jesus"* (27-57)

As evening approached, there came a rich man from Arimathea, named Joseph, who had himself become a disciple of Jesus. Going to Pilate, he asked for Jesus' body, and Pilate ordered that it be given to him. Joseph took the body, wrapped it in a clean linen cloth, and placed it in his own new tomb that he had cut out of the rock. He rolled a big stone in front of the entrance to the tomb and went away.

JOHN; *"The Burial of Jesus"* (19-38)

Later, Joseph of Arimathea asked Pilate for the body of Jesus. Now Joseph was a disciple of Jesus, but secretly, because he feared the Jews. With Pilate's permission, he came and took the body away.

At the place where Jesus was crucified, there was a garden, and in the garden a new tomb, in which no one had ever been laid. Because it was the Jewish day of Preparation and since the tomb was nearby, they laid Jesus there.

According to Matthew, a man called Joseph took the body and placed it in a new tomb which he had cut out of the rock.

According to John, Jesus had been crucified in a garden and in this garden there was a new tomb in which no one had ever been laid. Since it was the Jewish day of Preparation and the tomb was nearby, Joseph, who did not need to build a new tomb by cutting it out of rock, laid Jesus there in the garden.

My dear readers!

The divine book should belong only to Allah and there should be no addition by a human being, not even one word. I have examined the sections regarding the burial of Jesus, word by word. Unfortunately, I could not find a single word that belonged to Allah. Truly I am concerned about the true Bible because the legends about Joseph from Arimathea have been taken as the word of Allah, and are recited in the churches as the holy book and constitute the foundations of contemporary Christianity.

✱✱✱

Resurrection of Prophet Jesus According to the Christians:

MARK; *"The Resurrection"* (16-1)

When the Sabbath was over, Mary Magdalene, Mary the mother of James, and Salome bought spices so that they might go to anoint Jesus' body. Very early on the first day of the week, just after sunrise, they were on their way to the tomb and they asked each other, "Who will roll the stone away from the entrance of the tomb?" But when they looked up, they saw that the stone, which was very large, had been rolled away. As they entered the tomb, they saw a young man dressed in a white robe sitting on the right side, and they were alarmed. "Don't be alarmed," he said. "You are looking for Jesus the Nazarene, who was crucified. He has risen! He is not here.

LUKE; *"The Resurrection"* (24-1)

On the first day of the week, very early in the morning, the women took the spices they had prepared and went to the tomb. They found the stone rolled away from the tomb, but when they entered, they did not find the body of the Lord Jesus. While they were wondering about this, suddenly two men in clothes that gleamed like lightning stood beside them. In their fright the women bowed down with their faces to the ground, but the men said to them, "Why do you look for the living among the dead? He is not here; he has risen!"

There is no single word belonging to Allah in sections concerned with the resurrection of Prophet Jesus. They consist merely of legends or confusing narrations about the women who were looking for the body of their Lord Jesus.

If a Muslim girl from Konya, not Mary Magdalana, were to claim that she saw some men in the tomb and spoke to them, one's reaction would be that she had suffered an illusion. What if she happened to insist on what she saw? She would be probably advised to go to see a doctor! Let us look at other sections of the New Testament.

2- The Acts of Apostles

Luke, the writer of one of the four gospels, wrote the Acts of Apostles as well. In the first book, he narrated the events he had witnessed during the time of Prophet Jesus. In the second book, he conveys events that occurred after the death of Prophet Jesus. One may wonder if there is consistency between the Holy Book and the events that occurred after the death of Prophet Jesus, neither of which are words of Allah. I wonder, too, but no one investigates this question.

Let me give an example from this section.

"The Arrival at Rome (28-11)

After three months we put out to sea in a ship that had wintered in the island. It was an Alexandrian ship with the figurehead of the twin gods Castor and Pollux. We put in at Syracuse and stayed there three days. From there we set sail and arrived at Rhegium. The next day the south wind came up, and on the following day we reached Puteoli. There we found some brothers who invited us to spend a week with them. And so we came to Rome."

3- Epistles

There are 21 epistles written by Paul, Peter, John, Joseph and Judas to private persons or communities. We will skip the Epistles only to avoid making our topic too lengthy.

4- Revelation

It is suggested that John wrote this section. It consists completely of illusions, stories, legends and the like. Let me give an example how people degenerated the true Bible.

"The Woman and the Dragon" (12-1)

A great and wondrous sign appeared in heaven: a woman clothed with the sun, with the moon under her feet and a crown of twelve stars on her head. She was pregnant and cried out in pain as she was about to give birth. Then another sign appeared in heaven: an enormous red dragon with seven heads and ten horns and seven crowns on his heads. His tail swept a third of the stars out of the sky and flung them to the earth. The dragon stood in front of the woman who was about to give birth...

My dear readers!

The story goes on, but this excerpt is sufficient for the wise. Now, let us look at the views of moderate Christians regarding the Bible:

W. Graham Scroggie, the author of the book "Is the Bible the Word of God?" says:

"..Yes, the Bible is human, although some out of zeal, which is not according to knowledge, have denied this. Those books have passed through the minds of men, are written in the language of men, were penned by the hands of men and bear in their style the characteristics of men..."

Kenneth Cragg, an Anglican Bishop says:

"...Not so the New Testament...There is condensation and editing; there is choice reproduction and witness. The Gospels have come through the mind of the church behind the authors. They represent experience and history..."

IF THE TRUE BIBLE IS FOUND WHAT WILL HAPPEN?

*

In 1947, Bedouin shepherds found a collection of ancient scrolls that were stored in a pottery container in a cave near Jerusalem. This finding had a great impact on the Christian world and was long-debated. The media, including that in Turkey, announced this discovery in headlines, saying "True Bible Found." Christian authorities immediately began to examine the scrolls, yet they could not find anything regarding the accuracy of the Bible.

Is the true bible hidden?

L'Evenement Du Jeudi", a French magazine stated in its July issue of 1993:

"Now, it is time to reveal the real Bible, yet, some power centers hinder it since it may result in chaos for Christian Civilization."

What happens if the true Bible is revealed?

First, the true Bible abolishes the legend of the Trinity and it is revealed that Allah is one and that Prophet Jesus is the servant and the prophet of Allah, like all other prophets. It puts an end to the myths that Prophet Jesus was crucified and that God sacrificed his only son for the sins of humanity. It obliterates the status and authority of churches, thus discharging thousands of people like Galileo.

You remember: Galileo was excommunicated because he said that the earth revolved around sun. When he left court, he was sentenced, yet, he said to himself: "Nevertheless, it does move." In 1992, Pope John Paul revoked his excommunication after 350 years and declared that he was a sincere Christian, so that he might be saved.

If the true Bible were to be revealed, the Christian world, by the will of Allah, will believe in Prophet Muhammad, since his coming is openly expressed, and the world will have a new order.

The stories of Joseph from Arimathea, Mary Magdelena, the woman who cried out in pain in the sky and the red dragon with seven heads might have been interesting in the Middle Ages, but they are not persuasive or credible for today's Europe. The Qur'an is the only address that will scientifically and spiritually satisfy the entire Christian world and all of humanity. I believe and hope that the time when they meet with the Qur'an is close. Perhaps it is tomorrow, or closer than tomorrow.

THE CHARACTERISTICS OF THE DIVINE BOOK AND THE QUR'AN

*

One of the characteristics of the divine book is its language.

As the Qur'an has preserved its language as it was revealed to the Prophet, it maintains its status as the divine book. Otherwise, it could not be deemed a divine book. The divine books that have been translated into other languages cannot be called directly divine books. For example, the Qur'an translated into Turkish cannot be called the Qur'an, but rather the Turkish translation of the Qur'an.

It is clear that the Qur'an, the last divine book, has preserved its language as revealed to Prophet Muhammad. It is the only book that has preserved the status of divine book in terms of linguistics.

Another characteristic of the divine book is its syntax.

To maintain the syntax is to preserve the places and the word order that was determined by Allah. Let us look at different copies of the Qur'an. Beginning from the Mother Qur'an, written down in the era of Prophet Abu Bakr, let us take historical copies, including those copied by Prophet Uthman, one of which is exhibited in the Hermitage in St. Petersburg with the one being exhibited in Topkapi Palace, and contemporary copies printed in different countries. We can see that they all begin with Surah Fatiha and end with Surah An Nas, and the syntax is the same in all, that is it is the syntax determined by Allah.

The Qur'an is the only divine book in terms of lyrical structure, as well. The most important characteristic of the divine book is that it should belong to only Allah and contain no contribution from anyone other than Allah. If the words of the prophets or other people are added to divine books, they will no longer be divine and cannot be regarded as the main source of their religions.

Prophet Muhammad, the last prophet, prohibited his words from being written, allowing only the verses of the Qur'an to be written so that the Qur'an would not be changed. His words are known as Hadith and have not been added to the Qur'an. Saying "Amen" after reciting Surah Al-Fatiha is the practice of the Prophet, but this word has not been added to the Qur'an, because it is not the word of Allah, but the word of the Prophet.

The Qur'an is the only book that preserves the status of divinity.

A COMPARISON OF THE QUR'AN AND THE BIBLE

*

The Qur'an belongs only to Allah. There is no single word from Prophet Muhammad in the Qur'an. Whereas, contemporary Bibles do not contain even the words of Prophet Jesus, let alone the words of Allah.

For example:

JOHN; *The Death of Jesus* (28-30)

Later, knowing that all was now completed, and so that the Scripture would be fulfilled, Jesus said, "I am thirsty." 29A jar of wine vinegar was there, so they soaked a sponge in it, put the sponge on a stalk of the hyssop plant, and lifted it to Jesus' lips. 30When he had received the drink, Jesus said, "It is finished." With that, he bowed his head and gave up his spirit.

If this section, which contains 72 words, has only six words from Prophet Jesus: "I am thirsty" and "It is finished", who then expressed the other words? If these words belong to the witnesses, what do we call the Bible, the word of Allah or is it witnesses' testimony? Is it an inquiry or a theocratic history book?

The Acts of Apostles

The Acts of the Apostles in the Bible include the events that occurred in Christianity after the time of Prophet Jesus with his disciples. Anything written about events after Prophet Jesus has been added and they are the words of humans. When we look at the Qur'an, there is no single word regarding the rise of Islam or what the companions of the Prophet did after his death. It is clear that the Qur'an is the only book that preserves its divine status with no additions at all.

The Epistles

In the section known as The Epistles of the Bible, there are 21 letters that were written by Paul, Peter, John, Joseph and Judas to certain people and communities. These are clearly the words of humans and a latter addition to the Bible.

When we look at the Qur'an, it does not contain even a word from the letters written to kings and governors by Prophet Muhammad, let alone the letters written to other people and communities by the four caliphs and the Companions.

The accuracy of the epistles written by Paul, Peter, John, Joseph and Judas is still debated, because we do not know where their originals are or where they came from.

In year seven A.H., Prophet Muhammad sent the following letters:

A letter to the King of the Byzantines, Heraclius,

A letter to Chosroes, Emperor of Persia

A letter to the Negus, king of Abyssinia (Ethiopia)

A letter to the Vicegerent of Egypt, called Muqawqas

A letter to Harith bin Abi Shamir Al-Ghassani, King of Damascus

A letter to Haudha bin Ali, Governor of Yamama

He sent these letters with special envoys. Although some of the letters disappeared or were torn up, two of them, the letters to the Heraclius and Muqawqas, still exist in their original parchment form and can be seen in Topkapi Palace Museum and the Amman Museum. The text of the letters is as below:

In the Name of Allah, Most Gracious, Most Merciful.

From Muhammad servant of Allâh and His Messenger to Muqawqas, vicegerent of Egypt. Peace be upon him who follows true guidance. Thereafter, I invite you to accept Islam. Therefore, if you want security, accept Islam. If you accept Islam, Allâh, the Sublime, shall reward you doubly. But if you refuse to do so, you will bear the burden of the transgression of all the Copts.

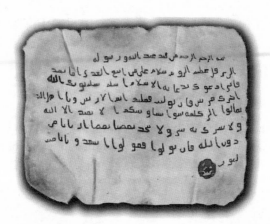

In the Name of Allah, Most Gracious, Most Merciful.

This letter is from Muhammad, the Servant of Allah and His Messenger to Heraclius the ruler of Byzantines. Peace be upon him who follows the right path. I invite you with the call of Islam. Accept Islam and you will find peace. Allah will double your reward. But if you turn away then you will have upon you the sin of Arisiyyin (his subjects)."

THE QUR'AN AND PROPHET MUHAMMAD

∗

Western scholars who have examined the lives of the Companions of Prophet Muhammad and who have compared the different copies of the Qur'an which were made at different times to the contemporary versions accept that the Qur'an is an original book which has undergone no changes at all.

Yet they have a doubt because of their fanaticism:

Let me try to show that the Qur'an is not the word of Prophet Muhammad with some examples of text from the Qur'an. I hope that when they read this, they will understand and benefit from it.

Example-1

"Glory be to Him Who created pairs of all things, of what the earth grows, and of their kind and of what they do not know."
(Ya-seen, 36)

Allah Almighty states that He created every kind of creature, human, ant, or elephant, in pairs; at the time when the Qur'an was revealed the people of this region, although they understood this to be true of the animals around them, had no idea how far the truth of this statement went.

People did not know about micro parasites until the microscope had been invented. They were not aware of the fact that different micro parasites surrounded their mouths, noses, and skins.

Allah Almighty informs us that He created all creatures in pairs. A spoon of water contains millions of micro parasites. They have also mouths, stomachs, digestive systems and reproductive organs.

What about inorganic entities?

The atom, which is the basic component of matter, consists of negatively charged electrons and positively charged protons, and revolves around a nucleus.

How mighty is Allah Who has created basic components of matter, the electrons and protons in pairs, as negative and positive!

Example-2

"And We have made the heaven a guarded canopy." *(Anbiya, 32)*

Allah Almighty protects sky against meteors with atmosphere, which is made up of gases that filter light and heat and which have no color, taste, or smell.

When meteors that fall from space enter into the atmosphere, they are burned up by the heat of 2000°C degree and are transformed into gases and dust. Furthermore, the ozone layer absorbs dangerous ultraviolet rays and thus protects the world. But how could people have understood this in the 7th century?

Example-3

"He (Allah) has made the two seas to flow freely (so that) they meet together: Between them is a barrier which they cannot pass." *(Ar-Rahman,19-20)*

While German scientists explored Bab el Mandeb, where the waters of the Aden Gulf and the Red Sea converge, they realized that waters of Red Sea and the Indian Ocean do not mix.

Likewise, the French oceanographer Cousteau found that the waters of the Atlantic Ocean and the Mediterranean Sea do not mix. When he was told that the Qur'an told us about this 1,400 years ago, Cousteau was very surprised.

Example-4

"And He it is Who created the night and the day and the sun and the moon; all (orbs) travel along swiftly in their celestial spheres."
(Anbiya, 33)

Allah Almighty informs us that He set up an order in the material world and created day and night by turning the earth in its orbit. He also created the sun and moon, which travel along in their celestial spheres.

Galileo was summoned before the ecclesiastical court when he declared that the world revolves around the sun. If the Pope had been aware of the Qur'an, he would not have excommunicated Galileo, imprisoning him until he turned blind.

Example-5

" What! now! and indeed you disobeyed before and you were of the mischief-makers!

But We will this day deliver you with your body that you may be a sign to those after you, and most surely the majority of the people are heedless to Our communications."
(Yunus, 91-92)

The Pharaoh was the bloodiest dictator of its time. When he was about to drown, he said: "I submit." Yet his testimony was not accepted and Allah said: "What! Now! And indeed you disobeyed before and you were of the mischief-makers. But We will this day deliver you with your body that you may be a sign to those after you, and most surely the majority of the people are heedless to Our communications."

While thousands of soldiers of Pharaoh were destroyed in Red Sea, the corpse of the Pharaoh was washed up on a hill on the shore. The Qur'an tells of this event, of which nobody was aware or had heard of before. The Qur'an, a genuine divine book, is not a legend, story or the word of humans. 1,400 years ago, it stated that the corpse of the Pharaoh was to be found on a hill on the shores of the Red Sea, and would be found to be a lesson for coming generations. 3,000 years after the Pharaoh's death, British researchers who were exploring the shores of the Red Sea, came across a puzzling situation. There was a man's corpse that had been preserved for many years. His flesh, hair and skin had not decayed and he was laying his face downwards like he was prostrating. Researchers took the corpse immediately for examination. Soon, they declared that this was the corpse of the Pharaoh, which was put on display in the British Museum.

We can give hundreds of examples like this from the Qur'an. Let us stop here and examine how the Qur'an cannot possibly be the word of Prophet Muhammad.

THE QUR'AN CANNOT BE THE WORD OF PROPHET MUHAMMAD

✳

Prophet Muhammad was born in the Arabian Peninsula in the 7th century. He grew up among cruel and semi-primitive people. He was illiterate. How can one claim that the Qur'an is his and insist that he was aware of the following things?

That plants and micro organisms were created in pairs;

That the atmosphere is a sort of ceiling protecting the earth from meteors;

That the ozone layer absorbs dangerous ultra-violet rays and protects the earth;

That the world, the sun and the moon travel along in their orbits;

That the waters of the different seas do not combine;

That the corpse of the Pharaoh, who drowned in the Red Sea in front of Prophet Moses and the children of Israel, would be found after 1,400 years on the shores of the Red Sea.

THE SPIRITUALITY OF THE QUR'AN
*

All books, including the most exciting novels and stories, will bore people if read over and over. This is not true for the Qur'an. Those who recite or listen to the Qur'an are never bored. For example, Muslims who perform the five daily prayers repeat Surah Al Fatiha forty times a day, but they are never bored. On the contrary, they find spiritual tranquility and peace.

If one recites the Qur'an according to the rules of Arabic recitation and pronunciation, they will have more reward, gain more tranquility and more joy. Because the rules of *tajwid* like *mad, izhar, ikhfa, idgam, gunna* and the stop signs are spiritual notes that ensure the correct recitation and constitute the natural rhythm and rhyme of the Qur'an.

If one diligently recites the Qur'an according to its spiritual notes in its natural rhyme, those who listen to them also attain spiritual joy and peace and the angels of compassion visit them.

One should recite the Qur'an accurately and correctly in order to attain the full benefit from it. One should also recite it in its original letters. The letters of the Qur'an do not have exact counterparts in other alphabets. So those who recite the Qur'an through phonetic transcription can make some errors.

The Qur'an, the last divine book, should be continuously recited and memorized to prevent it from being changed and so that it does not lose its authenticity, unlike the books that preceded it.

While before the Qur'an only the prophets memorized the divine texts, thousands of Companions memorized the Qur'an. After the Companions, the complete memorization of the Qur'an has continued until now. The world has always had tens of thousands of people who had memorized the Qur'an.

Today, Muslims who have not memorized the entire Qur'an know at least Surah Al Fatiha, and some short verses. They recite these verses both when praying and at other times and teach them to their children.

Our beloved Prophet said, "The best of you are those who learn the Qur'an and teach it to others." He also said, "One who recites one letter out of the Qur'an is rewarded ten times." *Basmala* (*Bismillahirrahmanirrahim*) has 19 letters. Thus if one recites the *basmala* once, they receive 190 rewards. One, who recites the *basmala* ten times gets 1,900 rewards.

As our children who are learning to memorize the Qur'an attain millions of rewards by repeating verses and pages their spiritual joy and tranquility increase. Their inner world is enlightened. They are apparent among their friends and are perceived as serene, calm and trustworthy individuals.

ISLAMIC CIVILIZATION
*

Before Islam, the Mecca pagans were mostly illiterate, living primitively and worshipping idols. They were alcoholics who ate carrion and drank the blood of the animals they slaughtered.

They did not know anything about hygiene, personal or otherwise. They were arrogant people who dressed in garments that were so long they swept the ground.

They were inhuman people who buried their daughters alive. They brought their daughters to the hole prepared before and pushed them in while looking on. When their daughters cried "Daddy, daddy" they paid no attention and buried them anyway.

When the revelation first came to Prophet Muhammad on Mount Nour, he began to shake and sweat. His forehead was covered with droplets like pearls.

He was the final messenger. He was to begin preaching the message from Mecca. Mecca was an unknown, because no prophet had appeared from there before Prophet Abraham went there.

This was not a decision he made himself, rather he was required to perform his mission.

He began with his beloved wife, Khadija. Then he turned to Abu Bakr, Ali, Zad, Uthman, Abdurrahman, Talha, Sa'd and Zubair, and they became the first Muslims. The number of his ummah was almost as great as the number of fingers on two hands.

He warned the semi-primitive pagans with the wrath of Hell and invited them to a belief in the unity of Allah. His situation resembled that of a lamb that warns the wolves when she sees hunters. He had no choice but to warn them as his compassion for his *ummah* was infinite. He could not bear for them to be cast into Hellfire.

These were monstrous people who had once buried their daughters alive, but now they became pioneers of good manners and set wonderful examples for others as they tasted true belief and conversation with Prophet Muhammad. They exhibited excellent examples for those who hated to live like pagans. They adopted Islam easily. Islam was growing, not only in Mecca, but also in Medina and in the tribes outside of Mecca.

THE FIRST SOCIAL ACTIVITY OF ISLAMIC STATE: MASJID

*

The emigration of Prophet Muhammad and the Meccan Muslims to Medina launched a new era; it was here that they founded first Islamic state. Before the emigration, the Muslims of Medina used to pray in different congregations, but after the arrival of our Prophet, they all wanted to pray in one congregation. This meant that a small mosque, a masjid, be built. Our Prophet decided to build a masjid with his Companions. They first established the location and began to build it. As construction continued, an event unparalleled in human history took place. Until that time, only slaves would work the construction jobs or other heavy tasks. The owners of slaves would watch from the shadows.

Although Prophet Muhammad was a prophet and leader, he began to dig with a spade along with the slaves; at first, they were bewildered, but then everybody began to work with the slaves.

When we think that in some parts of the world there is still discrimination based on race or religion, we can easily recognize the importance of the equality that Prophet Muhammad demonstrated 1,400 years ago.

The masjid built by the most distinguished people of the world, Prophet Muhammad and his Companions, was soon completed and opened for worship. The Muslims prayed there five times a day and they eagerly attended the conversations of the Prophet after prayers. The masjid was the only place for their social activities. Apart from praying five times a day, it was also the house of knowledge and culture and a symbol of cooperation, unity and a spirit of fellowship.

While the *ayats* (verses) of belief were generally revealed in Mecca, the *ayats* regarding the rules of Islam were revealed in Medina, and these were immediately put into action.

The Companions who matured spiritually and who were purified from sins and other bad habits through Conversations with Prophet Muhammad had become the most civilized people in the world in terms of hygiene.

Before Islam, they would not take baths for weeks; they stunk and they their skin was darker than normal, due to sweat and dirt. After they became Muslims, they frequently took baths (*guthl*) and smelt pleasant. When they made their ablutions for prayer five times a day, they washed their hands, faces and feet; they passed their wet hands over their heads (*mash*), and cleaned their mouths and noses.

Making ablutions five times a day was not an action performed anywhere else in the world at this time, which leads us to the conclusion that the first Muslims were in fact the most civilized and hygienic people of their time.

In addition, they used a natural tooth-brush called *miswak* to clean their teeth. It helped prevent decaying and made the teeth whiter, as well as preventing other oral diseases. Again, the Muslims were the first in the world to be concerned about oral hygiene.

Prophet Muhammad asked the Muslims to be clean, saying "Cleanliness is from Imaan (belief)." He advised them to wash their hands before and after meals, to cut their nails, to remove the hairs under their arms, to refrain from spitting in the streets and not to eat things that smelt heavily of garlic or onion when coming to the mosques.

He paid great attention to hygiene and spiritual cleanliness. He said: "Iman has over seventy branches, the uppermost of which is the declaration: 'None has the right to be worshipped but Allah'; and the least of which is the removal of harmful objects from the road." Hence, he introduced another first, voluntarily environmental cleanliness; as a result all the streets of Medina became clean.

The number of literate people in Medina was relatively less than that of Mecca. The people felt no need to learn as they were not interested in trade or literature. After the arrival of Prophet Muhammad, they were required to learn in order to read the Qur'an. In the second year of Hijra, seventy people of Mecca were captured during the Battle of Badr; they were told they could go free if they each taught ten people from Medina how to read and write. They worked hard to do so. Soon, these students began to teach their friends and all of the young people in Medina were soon able to read and write.

When the *ayats* regarding inheritance were revealed, there emerged a need for mathematics. Since the Qur'an declared that the shares of inheritance was 1/2, 1/4, 1/8, 2/3, 1/3, or 1/6, depending on the situation, education in mathematics was necessary to comply with these *ayats*. These people who had been illiterate not long before Islam quickly learnt mathematics and began to solve the problems of inheritance.

The *ayats* regarding prayers, fasting, *zakat* and the pilgrimage are related to the movement of the sun and the moon. Further, the examination of and thinking about the creation of the earth and skies are seen as forms of worship. Therefore, Muslims began to be interested in the science of astronomy. They observed the movements of the moon so that they could determine the times of the fast, the pilgrimage and the religious festivals. They also observed the movements of sun so that they could determine the times of the five daily prayers. They manufactured some clocks, including a sun clock and an alarm clock.

Harun Rashid, the Abbasid Caliph, sent an alarm clock to the French King, Charles I as a gift. When the clock rang when it was delivered, the King and his entourage kept away from it, assuming that had been possessed.

As the payment of *zakat* was incumbent upon Muslims, it helped to ensure social cooperation and financial collaboration. In addition to the payment of *zakat*, other means of charity (*ushr, fitr*, the sacrificing of animals) enhanced social cooperation and participation. The Prophet said: One who goes to sleep full while his neighbor is hungry is not of us." This ensured that everybody had shelter and food. The solidarity of Muslims was not mere words, it was sincere. When they met in the street, they greeted each other saying "*Assalamu Alaikum*-Peace upon you" and shook hands with each other. They visited the sick, solved the problems of those who were in trouble and helped orphans and widows. The leading Companions from the Aws and Hazraj tribes came together. They ate together and prayed in the same ranks.

HUMAN RIGHTS AND ISLAM

The Arabian Peninsula

Before Islam, as there was no single authority in the Arabian Peninsula, every tribe was autonomous. Every tribe had its own customs, traditions, chief and idols. Nobody could break the customs, violate the orders of the chief or worship any idol other than the idol of tribe.

Women had no rights of marriage or divorce. They had to marry or live with the person their parents or guardians decided upon.

They had no rights of ownership or inheritance, and no choice but to beg for a living if their husbands passed away.

Slaves were oppressed and insulted. They were dominated. They had to work hard without any pay or food. If they resisted, they faced death.

While the chiefs of tribes amused themselves with alcohol and female slaves, the people had to work hard to secure their basic needs and pay.

In the East:

In China Confucius was canonized, Buddha in India, Zerdust and Jamshid in Persia and statues were built of them.

The Indians sanctified cow, the river Ganges, while the Persians sanctified Lake Sawa; and began to worship these inanimate objects.

There was terrible discrimination among people. Dictators were seen to immortal. Rajas, nobles, and rich people were the upper classes and they were immune. Other people were miserable, downtrodden and exploited.

Women were seen to exist merely for the sexual satisfaction of men. Slaves were dominated and had to work hard and were put up in stables alongside animals.

The poor were financing the extravagance of the rich through heavy taxes. Those who could not afford to pay were imprisoned.

In the West:

The West was different from the East in

terms of belief. Its religion was Christianity, yet it was undergoing the darkest time of its history.

People were fighting against hunger and diseases. While there was shortage of bread, the kings and the lords in palaces and the priests in churches were enjoying luxuries.

The kings and lords extorted money from the people to cover their extravagances. The priests, too, forced people to come to the church and confessing, even fining them. While even kings and lords were threatened with excommunication, poor people were required to attend churches to confess and give all their earnings to the priests. However, the priests were not content. They began to sell parcels of heaven to the rich and became incredibly wealthy.

What about women and slaves? They were exploited to even a greater degree.

Some slaves were forced to work hard without any food or pay, while others were set to pull the oars, being whipped and mistreated.

Christianity, which was once a true religion, had now become deformed and a tool of exploitation. It was a cause for the masses to be mistreated and impoverished.

John W. Drapper, a historian says in this regard:

"Europe of that day was barbarian. Christianity did not civilize them. The Muslims in Spain taught them to wash, wear clean clothes, cut their nails and build toilets in their houses. "

Is Islam or Christianity a religion of the blood?

No! Neither Islam nor Christianity are a blood religion, because there can be no compulsion in religion. However, if religion becomes a tool of exploitation and oppression, then it becomes a blood religion.

Allah sent Prophet Muhammad as the final messenger, and this is clear evidence that Islam is not religion that is inherited. He lost his father before his birth, his mother at six and his grandfather at eight. He was destined to grow up an orphan, raised by his uncle and aunt. He was calm, quiet, polite and tranquil man. When it was revealed that he was the prophet on Mt.

Noor, he was not overly pleased. Instead, he was frightened and worried. Yet, it was not up to him. He had been sent as a prophet to all of humanity. His mission began in Mecca. His first believer was his beloved wife, Khadija. Then came Abu Bakr, Ali, Zaid, Uthman, Abd-ar-Rahman, Talha, Sa'd and Zubair. His ummah consisted of nine people, one woman and eight men. These companions were the first believers and the pioneers of Muslims in the hardest times. May Allah be pleased with them.

Prophet Muhammad first delivered his messages in secrecy. When he was ordered to deliver his message in public, he began to do so and caused a shock in Mecca.

The rulers of Mecca fiercely attacked him so that they could keep their positions and their regimes, which were based on idolatry. They insulted Prophet Muhammad and tortured newly converted Muslims. However, the tree of Islam planted by Prophet Muhammad began to produce fruit.

Although the rulers of Mecca increased their pressure, the numbers of Muslims also increased. Islam also spread among the tribes outside of Mecca.

Six people from Medina became Muslims in Aqaba after they met with Prophet Muhammad. Thus, Islam began to spread in Medina. Soon, most of the people in this city had converted to Islam and they invited Prophet Muhammad to their city. Prophet Muhammad accepted their invitation and the Muslims emigrated from Mecca to Medina. A new era began after Prophet Muhammad entered into Medina. Muslims passed from being a congregation to a state and the first Islamic state was established.

Beginning with a single person in Mecca, in 13 years Islam had moved to Medina and a new era had now begun. During that period, Prophet Muhammad had not wielded a needle, lest alone sword. All the converts had come to Islam by free will.

Founding a state or declaring independence is easier than maintaining independence or preserving the state. It was very difficult for the Islamic state, founded in a small city placed on the Arabian Peninsula, to sustain independence in the conditions of that time. The Islamic state was surrounded by hostile Jewish tribes, like the Banu Nadir, the Banu Quraiza and the Banu

Qainuqa, and hostile pagan tribes headed by the Meccans.

Neighboring tribes attacked Medina, taking animals and abducting people to sell in slave markets. It was necessary to maintain security in order for the Islamic State to survive not only in and around Medina, but also in the Arabian Peninsula.

Allah Almighty says:

"There is no compulsion in religion."

(Al-Baqara, 256)

Yes, there is no compulsion in the religion. People cannot be converted to Islam by force or intimidation. However, war is permissible to ensure the security of life and independence, which is the first priority of states.

When the Meccan pagans could not win in the battles of Badr and Uhud, they prepared an army of 10,000 men, consisting of Jews and pagans under the command of Abu Sufyan in the fifth year of the Hijrah. They marched against Medina to kill Prophet Muhammad and all the Muslims.

The Muslims dug deep trenches as a barrier against the invaders along the open parts of Medina, and engaged in a defensive battle using arrows and stones.

It was winter and cold. Furthermore, the Muslims' food stocks were exhausted.

As the battle developed, it did not go the way the pagans desired. They unsuccessfully tried to cross the trenches and wasted thousands of arrows for nothing.

At the time of the afternoon prayer on the last day of the battle, Archangel Gabriel came and informed the Muslims that the pagans would withdraw and that this the final attack of the Meccans against Medina.

In the evening a violent sandstorm accompanied by terrifying sounds came down on the camp of the Meccans.

This wind upset their cooking-pots and knocked over their tents. The animals rushed madly into their riders, their eyes burning with sand. The pagans, too, were made uneasy by the wind and could not see one another.

As the air darkened, the angels came to help and uttered the words "*Allah-u Aqbar*" in a roaring voice. The pagans were frightened and ran away.

The Battle of the Trench was the final defensive battle of the Muslims in Medina. After this battle, a period of conquests began. The Islamic State enlarged and conquered many places by the will of Allah Almighty.

The defeat of an army of 10,000 men was an important message for the enemies of the Muslims. Indeed, the Arab tribes understood this message very well and now paid attention to Islam. They sent committees to Medina and soon began to convert to Islam.

The Conquest of Mecca

The most important event in the era of Prophet Muhammad was the conquest of Mecca, because Mecca, the city of the Ka'ba, was the center of all the tribes that were opposed to Islam. Since the time of the attack of Abraha (before Prophet Muhammad was born) the importance of Mecca and Ka'ba had been well recognized.

The pagans in Mecca believed that if a Muslim army attempted to attack Mecca, its fate would be similar to that of the army of Abraha, which had been destroyed. The conquest of Mecca would actually be the conquest and Islamization of the Arabian Peninsula.

In the eighth year of the Hijrah, Prophet Muhammad surrounded Mecca. He headed an army of 10,000 men, all of whom were volunteers.

Before marching, he ordered his commanders not to attack anyone before they attacked and to avoid bloodshed.

He also sent a message to the people of Mecca, guaranteeing the lives of those who did not participate in the war, either entering the house of Abu Sufyan or the Ka'ba, or laying down arms, and locking their doors.

The Meccan pagans assumed that Prophet Muhammad would take revenge in return for what they had done, and therefore were fearful and anxious about what would happen.

When the conquest was completed accompanied by chants of *takbir*, Prophet Muhammad stood at the door of the Ka'ba and declared: "This day there is no reproof against you. Go your way, you are free..."

The Meccan people received this declaration with great joy and applause. They blamed themselves, since they had attributed bad names to Islam and Prophet Muhammad; they now began to convert o Islam.

Prophet Muhammad forgave the people of Mecca, who had been the greatest enemies of Islam, without condemning or punishing the, only stipulating that they should become Muslims. This was a manifestation of the personality of Prophet Muhammad and the essence of Islam. It is also clear proof that Islam is not a blood religion.

The Middle Ages were a time of darkness. People were without hope and unhappy. Those who were oppressed and mistreated yearned for a savior. They were humans and they had the right to live as humans.

As Allah had predestined, the Muslim armies came to rescue these oppressed people from the dictators. Those who had once perceived the Muslim armies as occupying forces and who had fought against them with dictators were perplexed by the good manners of Muslims. There was no discrimination in Islam on the basis of race, color or language. The poor and the rich, the boss and the worker were all equal. A slave could sit down with a noble of Quraiysh, they ate together and prayed in the same rank.

The Muslims did not exploit the places they conquered nor did they enslave people. Instead, they lifted the heavy taxes stipulated by dictators and issued a minimum tax called the *jizya*.

According to the order of Allah that there is no compulsion in the religion, no one was forced to convert to Islam. Yet, those who became acquainted with Islam and the Muslims voluntarily converted to Islam. Thus, the Islamic city state was transformed into a world state in a short time. If the Muslim armies had acted like occupying forces, shedding blood and compelling people to convert to Islam, then they would have faced intense resistance and probably would have failed with only a small group of Medina soldiers.

* * *

The year was 614 - A Persian army had conquered Jerusalem. Christian men, women and children, including those who had taken refuge in the churches, were killed. Churches were destroyed.

The year was 638 – Jerusalem was surrounded by Muslim army. The city surrendered to Caliph Umar without resistance. People were terrified, assuming that the horrific massacre committed 24 years before would happen again.

Umar proposed a treaty, saying that the people of Jerusalem were under the protection of Islam and that they were free and safe in their souls, their property, their churches, their crosses, the sick and the healthy, and their whole community.

He also lifted the heavy taxes stipulated by the Byzantines and issued a reasonable tax, the *jizya*.

Soon, the people of Jerusalem voluntarily began to convert to Islam.

The year was 1099 – Jerusalem was captured by the Crusaders. The Crusaders killed Muslim and Jewish inhabitants, including women, children, the sick and the poor - a total of 70,000. The streets of Jerusalem were full of dead bodies and blood.

The Crusades, the bloodiest religious wars in history, were eight wars originally sanctioned by Pope Urban II in the name of Christianity that continued from 1096-1270. The Crusades damaged not only the Muslims, but also the Jews and the Byzantines, who were Christians. Many places were sacked and millions of people were killed.

✳✳✳

The year was 1453 – On 29 May, a Tuesday, after the morning prayer, the Ottoman army entered Constantinople. The Byzantines were scattered around and most of them took refuge in Hagia Sophia. At noon, Sultan Mehmet, the Conqueror, along with his commanders and his teacher, entered the city from the gate of Topkapi and went to Hagia Sophia. Hagia Sophia was full of Byzantines, women and men, and they were crying loudly. Sultan Mehmed first prayed to thank Allah and then declared: "Stand up and do not cry! You have freedom in your religion and worship and you all are safe and secure."

✳✳✳

The year was 1492 – The Christians attacked the most beautiful mosque in the world, the Qartaba after defeating the Andulus State. They entered the mosque on horsebacd. They killed all the Muslims who had taken refuge in the mosque. They threw down the original copy of Qur'an that dated from the time of Claph Uthman and trampled upon it.

The Muslims and Jews in the Qartaba were forcibly converted to Christianity.

Bernard Shaw, a British writer, said:

"If there were only one religion for the world it would be Islam. Islam is the only religion, which can be adapted to every century. I predict that Islam will be the religion which will be accepted by tomorrow's Europe."

My dear readers!

Today's Bibles, which are dependent on dreams, legend and the testimonies of witnesses, are certainly the word of man. Since they cannot satisfy Europe in the present or in the future, by the will of Allah, the Europeans will accept Islam.

The fundamental basis of all true religions is unity, which is the belief that there is no god but Allah.

Those who associate a son to Allah are no different from those who worship idols.

Once, people worshipped the sun and moon. Today, this belief has no basis at all. Likewise, the legend that Prophet Jesus is the son of Allah and that Allah sacrificed His only son to save humanity is baseless. The baby lion, after growing up, becomes a mature lion and lives freely in the forests. A baby human, after growing up, becomes a mature human and lives freely. If Prophet Jesus were the son of Allah, he would become God (!) and create a new universe composed of hundreds of galaxies instead of dealing with only a few Jews in this small world.

We merely relate what is true and guidance is from Allah.

DER KORAN UND DIE BIBEL

IL CORANO E LA BIBBIA

EL CORÁN Y LA BIBLIA

Коран и Евангелие

LE CORAN ET LA BIBLE

Коран и Евангелие

ANGEL AND MAN

ENGEL UND MENSCHEN

ANGELO E UOMO

АНГЕЛ И ЧЕЛОВЕК

FIVE PEACES OF ADVICE FROM

БЕШ ТАFСИЯ

PET SAVJETA IZ ŽIVOTA IBRAHIMA BEN EDHEMA

www.tomorhoca.com